by Stuart Schwartz and Craig Conley

Consultant:
Karen Wagner
Manager
Mankato WorkForce Center

COLONIAL FORGE HIGH SCHOOL
550 COURTHOUSE ROAD
STAFFORD, VA 22554

Capstone Books

an imprint of Capstone Press
Mankato, Minnesota

Capstone Books are published by Capstone Press
151 Good Counsel Drive, P.O. Box 669, Mankato, Minnesota 56002
http://www.capstone-press.com

Copyright © 1999 Capstone Press. All rights reserved.
No part of this book may be reproduced without written permission from the publisher. The publisher takes no responsibility for the use of any of the materials or methods described in this book, nor for the products thereof.
Printed in the United States of America.

Library of Congress Cataloging-in-Publication Data
Schwartz, Stuart, 1945–
  Networking to find a job/by Stuart Schwartz and Craig Conley.
  p. cm.—(Looking at work)
  Includes bibliographical references and index.
  Summary: Discusses the development, use, and improvement of networking skills in order to find a job.
  ISBN 0-7368-0180-4
  1. Job hunting—Juvenile literature. 2. Social networks—Juvenile literature. [1. Job hunting. 2. Social networks. 3. Vocational guidance.] I. Conley, Craig, 1965–. II. Title. III. Series: Schwartz, Stuart, 1945– Looking at work.
HF5382.7.S394   1999
650.1—dc21   98-47357
                                                                             CIP
                                                                             AC

Editorial Credits
Carrie A. Braulick, editor; Steve Christensen, cover designer; Sheri Gosewisch
    and Kimberly Danger, photo researchers

Photo Credits
David F. Clobes, 6, 8, 10, 14, 16, 18, 20, 22, 24, 26
Photophile/Jeff Greenberg, 12
PhotoBank, Inc./4
Uniphoto/Lawrence Ruggeri, cover

Table of Contents

Chapter 1 Networking 5
Chapter 2 Benefits of Networking 7
Chapter 3 Creating a Network..................... 9
Chapter 4 Developing a Network............. 11
Chapter 5 Joining Groups 13
Chapter 6 Networking Meetings 15
Chapter 7 Helping Contacts...................... 17
Chapter 8 Overcoming Shyness................ 19
Chapter 9 Using the Telephone 21
Chapter 10 Using the Internet 23
Chapter 11 Effective Communication 25
Chapter 12 Following Up........................... 27

Words to Know... 28
To Learn More 29
Useful Addresses 30
Internet Sites 31
Index 32

Chapter 1

Networking

Job seekers find work in many ways. Some look at employment advertisements in newspapers. These ads tell about businesses that want to hire people. Other job seekers learn about jobs at employment agencies. Workers at these offices give people information about jobs. Some job seekers visit with other people who may help them find jobs. This is called networking.

Job seekers network with as many people as possible. These people are called contacts. Job seekers gain information about jobs from contacts.

Job seekers network with contacts in many ways. Job seekers and contacts communicate through personal meetings, telephone calls, and letters. Some job seekers and contacts communicate on the Internet. This system allows people to share information with others through computers.

Job seekers visit with others who may help them with their job searches.

Chapter 2

Benefits of Networking

Networking can benefit job seekers in many ways. Many job seekers who network find jobs that have not been advertised. Contacts may tell job seekers of job openings. Job seekers may find jobs where they can use their special skills or education. Many job seekers who network find jobs that fit their needs and interests.

Networking also can help job seekers improve their skills. For example, job seekers can improve their speaking and listening skills.

Networking also helps employers. These people or companies hire and pay workers. Employers sometimes meet the job seekers who network. Employers learn about these job seekers' skills and abilities. They may even decide to hire these job seekers. This saves employers time and money. They do not have to advertise to find workers.

Employers can save time and money when they hire job seekers who network.

Chapter 3

Creating a Network

Job seekers who network form groups of contacts. These groups become networks. People in these groups share information with each other.

Many job seekers make lists to help them create networks. They write down names of people who might help them find jobs. Networks can include friends, relatives, neighbors, and classmates. Teachers, club members, and employers also can be included in networks.

Job seekers share information with the contacts in their networks. They tell contacts about their job interests and skills.

Contacts may know other people who can help job seekers find jobs. Job seekers ask contacts for the names of these people. These names are called referrals. Job seekers use referrals to gather more information about jobs.

Many job seekers make lists of contacts to help them create networks.

Chapter 4

Developing a Network

Job seekers continue to add new contacts to their networks. Large networks make it easier for job seekers to find jobs.

Some job seekers do volunteer work to meet new contacts. Volunteers work for free. For example, job seekers can volunteer to help homeless people at shelters.

Job seekers may visit employment agencies. Workers at employment agencies may help job seekers find contacts in job areas that interest them.

Job seekers also find contacts through other ways. They attend speeches related to their job interests. They visit personnel departments at businesses. Workers in these offices help hire people to work at their businesses.

Many people job seekers meet may be contacts. Job seekers may talk to people next to them in grocery store lines. They may visit with people sitting near them on buses.

Job seekers may visit personnel departments to find contacts.

Chapter 5

Joining Groups

Many job seekers join groups related to their job interests. These groups help job seckers find contacts and learn about certain job areas.

Schools often have groups that job seekers can join. For example, they may have computer or science clubs. Many school groups help prepare their members to work in certain job areas.

Groups help job seekers find contacts in many ways. For example, school and community groups may invite employers to speak at meetings. They may tour companies. Groups may have lists of employers.

Job seekers who join groups should be active members. They should work with other members to meet the groups' objectives. Job seekers meet as many group members as possible. They listen carefully to the members. They tell other members about their job interests.

Groups can help job seekers learn more about job areas that interest them.

Chapter 6

Networking Meetings

Many job seekers choose to meet personally with their contacts. Job seekers gather important information at networking meetings. These meetings sometimes are called informational interviews.

Many job seekers arrange meetings with employers. Job seekers may call employers to arrange meetings. They also may send letters.

These meetings sometimes are social. For example, job seekers and employers may meet at restaurants. Other meetings are professional. These meetings may be at employers' business places. Most networking meetings last about 20 to 30 minutes.

Job seekers ask contacts for advice at meetings. They may ask which job positions best fit their skills and interests. They may ask about places to look for jobs. Job seekers also make sure to ask contacts for referrals.

Job seekers ask contacts many questions at meetings.

Chapter 7

Helping Contacts

Contacts help job seekers find jobs. But job seekers also can help their contacts. For example, job seekers may find information about certain job areas. They may share this information with contacts. They may tell contacts where they found the information. Job seekers also may share the names of groups contacts can join.

Many job seekers who help contacts are rewarded. They may become friends with their contacts. Contacts may give job seekers referrals. They may let job seekers know about job opportunities that arise.

Good job seekers listen carefully to their contacts. They want to learn all they can about job opportunities. They also listen for ways to help their contacts.

Job seekers can help contacts in many ways.

Chapter 8

Overcoming Shyness

Not all job seekers find networking easy. Some job seekers are not comfortable talking with others. They may be shy or nervous. But there are ways to overcome these feelings.

Many job seekers prepare before they network. They may make scripts. These job seekers write down what they plan to say to contacts before they call them.

Some job seekers use their scripts to practice networking. They practice asking questions with friends or relatives. They also practice listening closely to others.

Some job seekers are shy around strangers. These job seekers can ask people they know to be contacts. Many job seekers feel more comfortable talking with people they know.

Job seekers may want to find information about contacts. For example, they can find out about contacts' interests. This information helps job seekers get to know their contacts.

Some job seekers practice asking questions and listening with friends or relatives.

Chapter 9

Using the Telephone

Telephones are important tools for job seekers. Job seekers use telephones for many different reasons.

Job seekers use telephones to arrange networking meetings. They introduce themselves to contacts. Job seekers also tell contacts why they are calling. If they were referred, job seekers tell contacts who gave the referrals.

Job seekers use telephones for interviews. They sometimes have telephone interviews when networking meetings are not possible. Telephone interviews usually are shorter than personal meetings. Most telephone interviews take less than 15 minutes.

Job seekers also use telephones to keep in touch with contacts after meetings. They may tell contacts about advances they made in their job searches. They may ask contacts more questions about certain job areas.

Many job seekers use telephones to arrange networking meetings.

Chapter 10

Using the Internet

The Internet is a quick and easy way for job seekers to communicate with contacts. Job seekers sometimes use the Internet instead of telephones.

Many job seekers use e-mail to send messages to contacts on the Internet. E-mail is a short word for electronic mail. Job seekers can use e-mail when networking meetings are not possible. They may send messages to contacts in other cities, states, and countries through e-mail.

Job seekers may send information to contacts in Internet discussion groups. These groups are sorted into individual subjects. For example, there are discussion groups about cars, animals, and movies. Job seekers can find discussion groups about their job interests. They use e-mail to send messages or questions to contacts in these groups. Many contacts then reply to job seekers by e-mail.

The Internet allows job seekers to easily communicate with their contacts.

Chapter 11

Effective Communication

Good communication skills are important for job seekers who network. They share information about their job interests with many contacts.

Job seekers need to speak clearly. Some job seekers practice their speaking skills. They may tape-record themselves to make sure they are speaking slowly and clearly.

Job seekers who network also need good writing skills. Their letters and e-mail messages to contacts should not have mistakes. All words should be spelled correctly. Job seekers can have someone review their letters or e-mail messages. This helps them make sure the information is correct and clear.

Job seekers who network also need to listen closely. This helps them gather information. Job seekers can practice listening with people they know. They may practice listening to teachers at school or family members.

Job seekers make sure their written information to contacts is correct and clear.

Chapter 12

Following Up

Job seekers who network follow up with their contacts. They thank contacts after meeting with them. They keep in touch with contacts by calling or writing to them.

Job seekers who network follow up meetings with thank-you letters. These letters thank contacts for their time and effort. They describe what job seekers learned from the meetings. The letters include job seekers' names, addresses, and telephone numbers. Contacts may want to locate job seekers in the future.

Many job seekers keep in touch with contacts. They may tell contacts interesting facts about their job searches. This can help contacts remember job seekers if they learn about job openings.

Contacts feel valued when job seekers follow up. Job seekers also may learn new information. Following up helps job seekers find satisfying jobs.

Job seekers write thank-you letters to their contacts after networking meetings.

Words to Know

communication (kuh-myoo-nuh-KAY-shuhn)—sharing information, ideas, or feelings with other people

contact (KON-takt)—a person who may help a job seeker find a job

employer (em-PLOI-ur)—a person or company that hires and pays workers

informational interview (in-fur-MAY-shuh-nuhl IN-tur-vyoo)—an interview to gain information about jobs

Internet (IN-tur-net)—a system that allows people to share information with others through computers

network (NET-wurk)—a group of people who share information with each other

referral (ri-FUR-uhl)—the name of a person who might be a contact; some job seekers ask contacts for a referral.

To Learn More

Marler, Patty and Jan B. Mattia. *Networking Made Easy.* Lincolnwood, Ill.: VGM Career Horizons, 1998.

Richardson, Douglas B. *Networking.* The National Business Employment Weekly Premier Guides. New York: Wiley, 1994.

Schwartz, Stuart and Craig Conley. *Finding Work.* Looking at Work. Mankato, Minn.: Capstone High/Low Books, 1998.

Schwartz, Stuart and Craig Conley. *Interviewing for Information.* Looking at Work. Mankato, Minn.: Capstone High/Low Books, 1999.

Useful Addresses

Human Resources Development Canada
140 Promenade du Portage, Phase IV
Hull, QC K1A 0J9
Canada

National Career Development Association
4700 Reed Road, Suite M
Columbus, OH 43220

U.S. Department of Labor
Office of Public Affairs
200 Constitution Avenue NW
Room S-1032
Washington, DC 20210

Internet Sites

America's Career InfoNet
http://www.acinet.org/acinet/resource

Canada WorkInfoNet
http://www.workinfonet.ca

Cornell Career Services
http://www.career.cornell.edu/ccs/
   CareerExploration/Networking

National Career Development Association
http://www.ncda.org

Index

advertisements, 5

education, 7
e-mail, 23, 25
employers, 7, 9, 13, 15
employment agencies, 5, 11

groups, 9, 13, 17, 23

informational interviews, 15
Internet, 5, 23

job openings, 7, 27

letters, 5, 15, 25, 27

meetings, 5, 13, 15, 21, 23, 27
mistakes, 25

networks, 9, 11

opportunities, 17

personnel departments, 11

referrals, 9, 15, 17, 21
relatives, 9, 19

schools, 13
scripts, 19
skills, 7, 9, 15, 25
speeches, 11
strangers, 19

telephones, 21, 23

volunteer work, 11